SINGAPORE

NICOLA BARBER

WORLD ALMANAC® LIBRARY

Please visit our web site at: www.worldalmanaclibrary.com
For a free color catalog describing World Almanac® Library's list of high-quality books and multimedia programs, call 1-800-848-2928 (USA) or 1-800-387-3178 (Canada). World Almanac® Library's fax: (414) 332-3567.

Library of Congress Cataloging-in-Publication Data

Barber, Nicola.
    Singapore / by Nicola Barber.
        p. cm. — (Great cities of the world)
    Includes bibliographical references and index.
    ISBN 0-8368-5047-5 (lib. bdg.)
    ISBN 0-8368-5207-9 (softcover)
    1. Singapore—Juvenile literature. I. Title. II. Series.
    DS609.B38   2005
    959.57—dc22   2004057607

First published in 2005 by
World Almanac® Library
330 West Olive Street, Suite 100
Milwaukee, WI 53212 USA

Produced by Discovery Books
Editors: Valerie Weber and Kathryn Walker
Series designers: Laurie Shock, Keith Williams
Designer and page production: Keith Williams
Photo researcher: Rachel Tisdale
Diagrams: Keith Williams
Maps: Stefan Chabluk
World Almanac® Library editorial direction: Mark J. Sachner
World Almanac® Library editor: Gini Holland
World Almanac® Library art direction: Tammy West
World Almanac® Library graphic design: Scott M. Krall
World Almanac® Library production: Jessica Morris

Photo credits: AKG Images: p. 27; Corbis/Jose Fuste Raga: p. 37; Corbis: p. 4; Corbis/Dallas and John Heaton: p. 38; Corbis/Reuters: p. 18; Eye-Ubiquitous/John Dakers: pp. 10, 24, 34, 41, 42; Getty Images/Travel Pix: cover and title page; Getty Images/Imagebank: p. 32; Getty Images/Kazuhiro Nogi: p. 13; Getty/AFP/Roslan Rahman: pp. 14, 29; Getty Images/Alfred Hind Robinson: p. 11; Hutchison/Robert Aberman: p. 39; Hutchison/Andrew Eames: p. 23; Hutchison/Jeremy Horner: p. 26; James Davis Travel: pp. 17, 22, 31; Panos/Jean-Leo Dugast: p. 16; Popperfoto: p. 12; Topham Picture Point: p. 8; Trip: pp. 7, 21; Trip/Tibor Bognar: p. 15; Trip/R.Nichols: p. 25.

Cover caption: At Singapore's riverfront, the giant skyscrapers of the business district tower over the old buildings of the Boat Quay—now a vibrant restaurant and entertainment strip.

Printed in Canada

1 2 3 4 5 6 7 8 9 09 08 07 06 05

Contents

Introduction 4

Chapter 1 History of Singapore 8

Chapter 2 People of Singapore 14

Chapter 3 Living in Singapore 22

Chapter 4 Singapore at Work 32

Chapter 5 Singapore at Play 38

Chapter 6 Looking Forward 42

Time Line 44

Glossary 45

Further Information 46

Index 47

Introduction

A vital trading post for hundreds of years, Singapore today is an island city-state off the southern tip of the Asian mainland. Though many peoples, such as the Malays, various other Southeast Asian powers, and the British, have ruled it throughout the centuries, it became an independent nation in 1965. Although Singapore has few natural resources apart from its strategic position, its booming economy gives it the second highest standard of living in Asia today (after Japan). This economic miracle, achieved since independence, is partly the result of strong government and partly due to its hard-working population.

Singapore is truly a multi-ethnic community with Chinese, Malay, Indian, and Eurasian populations. Since

◄ *Modern high-rise buildings mingle with traditional architecture in Singapore's Central Business District.*

independence, Singapore's government has promoted a strong sense of national identity, meaning that most people think of themselves first as Singaporeans and second as whatever their ethnic group is. Yet alongside this Singaporean identity, the differences between the various ethnic groups continue to be celebrated in food, language, religion, festivals, and many other ways.

Singapore is a beautiful city. At its center stand many older buildings, such as City Hall, Old Parliament House, and Raffles Hotel, which survive from the days when Singapore was a British colony. Modern skyscrapers, however, such as the towers of Raffles Place in the financial district, dominate the city's skyline. Its unique mixture of east and west cultures and of traditional and modern architecture attracts millions of tourists from all over the world every year.

Geography

Consisting of one large main island and about sixty tiny islands, Singapore lies off the southernmost tip of the Malay Peninsula. Its area is constantly growing because landfill is being added to coastal areas, reshaping the coastline in many places. From north to south, the maximum distance of Singapore's main island is 14 miles (23 kilometers); from east to west, it is 26 miles (42 km). The Strait of Johor separates the main island from Malaysia on the north; two causeways cross the strait. To the north is a highway called the

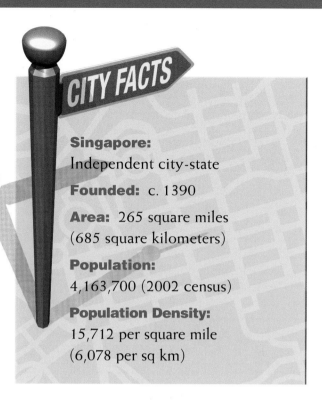

CITY FACTS

Singapore: Independent city-state

Founded: c. 1390

Area: 265 square miles (685 square kilometers)

Population: 4,163,700 (2002 census)

Population Density: 15,712 per square mile (6,078 per sq km)

Woodlands Causeway, to the west is a second, newer link at Tuas.

Singapore's center stands in the central southern part of the island, around the mouth of the Singapore River. To the south of the river lies the financial district and Chinatown, the area originally set apart for the Chinese community. Now the center of government and of the Supreme Court, the remaining colonial part of the city stands on the river's northern bank. Centers of the Indian and Malay communities, Little India and Kampong Glam bustle north of this area. With huge shopping malls, the main commercial part of the city stretches westward along Orchard Road.

Singapore has a gently undulating landscape, with its highest point at Bukit Timah 535 feet (163 meters) just west of the city center. Less than 2 percent of the

Singapore

City Center

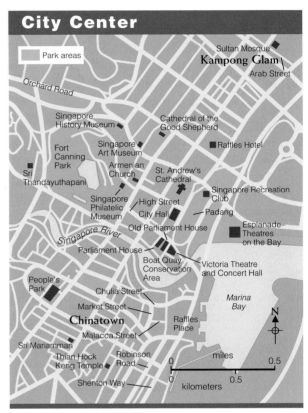

land is used for any form of farming. Tropical plants once covered the island, but most have been cleared to make way for buildings. About 5 percent of the land is still forested, mostly within Singapore's two nature reserves, Central Catchment Nature Reserve and Bukit Timah, both in the center of Singapore. On the northwest coast, the Sungei Buloh Nature Park contains some of the few remaining areas of mangrove swamp along Singapore's coastline. The mangroves provide an important habitat for many different species of bird.

Singapore's Small Islands

Singapore's offshore islands range from tiny coral outcrops to the larger islands such as Sentosa off the southern coast and on the northeast, Pulau Ubin and Pulau Tekong, which, at 9 square miles (24 square kilometers), is the largest. Many of these islands offer the people of Singapore a place for recreation and rest. Muslims and Chinese Taoists make pilgrimages to Kusu

Island, while Pulau Subar Darat and Pulau Subar Laut, known as the Sisters' Islands, are Singaporeans' favorites for swimming, diving, and snorkeling. Pulau Ubin offers the chance to see what Singapore was like in past centuries because it still has its traditional Malay fishing villages, called *kampung*. Today, the fishermen of Pulau Ubin mainly run prawn farms, providing these shrimplike crustaceans to the markets and restaurants of Singapore.

Singapore's Climate

Singapore lies 85 miles (137 km) north of the equator and therefore has a tropical climate—hot and humid with little variation

Many Languages

Malay is Singapore's national language, but English, Mandarin Chinese, and Tamil are all also official languages. English is the language of government and international business, but many Singaporeans also speak Singlish, a unique Singaporean dialect that combines English with Chinese and Malay words and grammar. The official Chinese dialect in Singapore is Mandarin (the official language of China), but many Chinese Singaporeans speak other Chinese dialects such as Hakka and Cantonese. The government, however, has been actively promoting Mandarin to replace these dialects.

▲ *Very few Malay fishing villages, or kampung, remain in Singapore. The wooden houses are built on stilts above the water.*

throughout the year. The average daily temperature is 81° Fahrenheit (27° Celsius), and the average humidity (the amount of moisture in the air) is between 80 and 85 percent. Rain falls throughout the year, but two monsoon seasons also bring heavier rain. From December to March, monsoons sweep in from the northeast, and, from June to September, they bring rains from the southwest. Thunderstorms are common throughout the year, particularly in the early evening.

CHAPTER 1

History of Singapore

Singapore's position in the middle of one of the world's richest trading routes, between the South China Sea and the Indian Ocean, led to its early growth. Tamil merchants from India and Chinese traders sailed through the Strait of Malacca, their boats loaded with spices, such as pepper, nutmeg, cinnamon, and ginger, as well as rice, silks, sandalwood, and tortoiseshell. As early as the second century A.D., the Greek astronomer and geographer Ptolemy identified a trading center called Sabara near modern-day Singapore.

In the third century, Chinese sailors described a place called Pu-Luo-Chung, meaning "island at the end of the peninsula," which could have referred to Singapore. Historians believe that people of Malay origin settled the island and that there was a settlement known as Temasek ("Sea Town"). The Italian explorer Marco Polo may have stopped at Temasek on his way from China to Sumatra in 1295. The first written record referring to Temasek, however, appears in Javanese court records of 1365, dating from the time when the island came under the power of the Javanese kingdom of Majapahit.

◄ *This painting from about 1850 portrays a view of Singapore's town and harbor from Government Hill, then the site of a botanical garden. Today, the area is known as Fort Canning Park.*

"A very large and noble city on the island of Malayur."

—Marco Polo on his way to Sumatra in 1295, probably referring to Temasek as Singapore was known at the time.

Pirate Haven, Then Obscurity

During the fourteenth and fifteenth centuries, Temasek became well known as a haunt for pirates who attacked the loaded ships that passed by. Singapore may have been founded by a young ruler called Iskandar from Palembang, part of the Srivijayan Empire based in Sumatra. He fled to Temasek in 1390, and the name Singapura dates from this time. However, Iskandar was driven out of Singapura. The following century, the small island settlement faded into obscurity and the rain forest. During the seventeenth century, the river people, who lived among the creeks and swamps of the islands, and the *orang laut*, sea nomads who traded with passing ships—inhabited the island. In the early years of the nineteenth century, a small band of Malays settled on the site of old Singapura.

European Traders and Thomas Raffles

During the early sixteenth century, Europeans began looking for ways to get direct access to the spice trade in the East. The Portuguese captured Malacca on the west coast of Malaya in 1511, and the Dutch took control of Malacca and Indonesia in 1641. By the beginning of the nineteenth century, the British East India

The "Lion City"

Singapura (Singapore) is Sanskrit for "Lion City," but no one truely knows how Singapore got this name. One version comes from the Sejarah Melayu (Malay Annals), a literary history of the Malays and their rulers during the fifteenth and early sixteenth centuries. According to this account, a king called Sang Nila Utama, from the great Sumatran empire of Srivijaya, took refuge on the island during a terrible storm. When he came across a strange creature with a red body, a black head, and a white breast, a companion told him that it was a lion. For this reason, Sang Nila Utama named the island Singapura. (Lions, however, have never lived on Singapore Island; it was probably a tiger.)

Company was challenging the Dutch for trade in the region.

Although the British held Bencoolen on the western side of Sumatra and Penang on the western coast of Malaya, they wanted to establish a base from which to control the Strait of Malacca. On January 29, 1819, Thomas Stamford Raffles, an officer of the British East India Company, landed on the island of Singapore. He found a landscape thick with rain forest and swamps, with one small village. Including the river people and sea nomads, about one thousand people lived on the island. Only a week later, on February 6, 1819, Raffles signed a treaty with the local Malay ruler allowing the

British East India Company to establish a trading base on the island.

The Dutch contested Raffles' acquisition, but in 1824, the British and the Dutch governments signed an agreement that gave Penang, Malacca, and Singapore, known as the British Straits Settlements, to Great Britain. Raffles did not stay in Singapore, visiting it only three times, but he oversaw its development under the first official British representative in Singapore, Colonel William Farquhar. To encourage ships to use the new port, Raffles made Singapore a free port with no restrictions or taxes on trade. He also urged immigrants from the Malay Peninsula, Sri Lanka, China, and elsewhere to come to provide manpower for clearing the rain forest, construction work, and trade. Raffles laid out the guidelines for the development of the settlement, including separate areas for the Malay, Chinese, and Indian communities. These communities are still found in present-day Singapore and are known as Kampong Glam, Chinatown, and Little India respectively.

Growth

Raffles left Singapore for the last time in 1823. The population increased rapidly, from fewer than a thousand people in 1819 to nearly one hundred thousand by 1870. Although pirate attacks were a major problem, trade also expanded. Singapore benefited from the opening of the Suez Canal in Egypt in 1869, which made the sea route between east and west considerably

▲ This statue of Sir Stamford Raffles, the founder of modern Singapore, stands by the Singapore River near the spot where it is believed he first landed in 1819. In the background are the skyscrapers of Raffles Place.

▲ *In this photograph from 1885, wooden boats are moored along Singapore's waterfront.*

shorter and less hazardous than before. More trading ships steamed into harbor. Then in 1888, a British botanist called H. N. Ridley brought rubber seedlings from South America and persuaded Malay farmers to grow them. Rubber and tin from mines in Malaya soon became major exports from Singapore.

Chinese Influence

By the beginning of the twentieth century, Singapore was a major world trading center. Problems arose, however, as Chinese immigrants began to form an ever larger part of Singapore's population. The Chinese were affected by events in their home country, where, in 1911, Chinese warlords began fighting for control of the nation. Chinese Nationalists and Communists initially allied against the warlords but by 1926 were fighting each other. Fearful of the influence of Communism, the British government in Singapore shut down Chinese schools during the 1920s and limited immigration from China—the first time immigration had been restricted in the colony.

"The city of Singapore was not built up gradually, the way most cities are. . . . It was simply invented one morning early in the nineteenth century by a man looking at a map."

—J. G. Farrell, author, from *The Singapore Grip*, 1978.

World War II

World War II was a turning point in the history of Singapore. In 1941, Japan invaded Malaya. The British assumed that any attack on Singapore would come from the sea and were unprepared for the Japanese forces that attacked from the Malay Peninsula on February 8, 1942. The British commander was forced to surrender to the Japanese, and Singapore was occupied and renamed Syonan-To, meaning "Light of the South." Thousands of civilians and prisoners of war were held in Changi Prison and other camps, and Japanese secret police killed thousands of Chinese Singaporeans. By the time the Japanese surrendered in 1945, over 100,000 civilians had died in Singapore.

▲ *Japanese soldiers armed with rifles and bayonets guard captured British soldiers in Singapore in 1942.*

Merdeka

The British took control of Singapore once again after World War II, but the political climate had changed and residents began to demand independence. Within a year, the British ended military rule of the British Straits Settlements and introduced some measure of self-government. The Federation of Malaya was formed, and Singapore became a separate crown colony, over

"The strongest bastion east of the Suez."

—Description of the supposed defenses of Singapore before the Japanese attack in 1942.

Lee Kuan Yew

Lee Kuan Yew (pictured above) was born in Singapore in 1923. He was educated at Raffles College in Singapore and at Cambridge University in England. Trained to be a lawyer, Lee Kuan Yew helped to found the People's Action Party in 1954. In 1959, he became the first prime minister of Singapore. Under his leadership, the PAP won the next eight general elections. Lee Kuan Yew stepped down as prime minister in 1990, although he remains a powerful figure as a senior cabinet minister in Singapore's government.

". . . if I say we are going in a certain direction . . . if you set out to block me, I will take a bulldozer and clear the obstruction."

—Lee Kuan Yew on his attitude to governing Singapore.

which Britain kept some control. For many, however, this was not enough. In 1955, the People's Action Party (PAP) was founded, led by a lawyer called Lee Kuan Yew. The slogan of the party was Merdeka, or "Independence." In the 1959 elections, the PAP won the majority of seats; it has held power in Singapore ever since.

Lee insisted on a merger with Malaya, but many people in Malaya feared the influence of the large Chinese population in Singapore. At the time of the merger in 1963, Malaya also absorbed the British colonial states of Sabah and Sarawak, both with Malay populations, as a balance for the Chinese population of Singapore, to form the Federation of Malaysia. Conflict within the federation, however, led to race riots between Malays and Chinese in 1964, and Singapore was expelled from Malaysia in 1965.

An Independent Nation

The outlook looked bleak for the newly independent state of Singapore. Under the leadership of Lee Kuan Yew, however, Singapore built a multiracial society held together by a strong sense of personal identity as Singaporeans. The economy also flourished, thanks to careful planning and a strong, stable government.

CHAPTER 2

People of Singapore

Singapore is a truly multi-ethnic society. About 77 percent of the population is Chinese, 14 percent is Malay, and 8 percent is Indian. The remainder of the population is made up mostly of Eurasians, people of mixed Asian and European descent. A large foreign population also lives in Singapore. Many immigrants have jobs in the finance and high-tech industries; others take on jobs in areas such as construction and housekeeping in houses and hotels, which many Singaporeans are unwilling to do.

Chinese Singaporeans

Singapore's Chinese population originally came from many different regions in China. The largest group is the Hokkiens from Fujian Province in southern China. The other groups are the Teochews who originally came from the Shantou region of Guangdong, the Cantonese from Guangzhou and Hong Kong, Hakkas from central China, and Hainanese from the island of Hainan in the South China Sea. The Chinese population in Singapore speaks a variety of dialects, but their common link is Mandarin Chinese, the language that is spoken in the Beijing area of

◄ *Singaporeans cross at a downtown intersection. Singapore is one of the wealthiest cities in the world, with a multiracial heritage that has given it a cosmopolitan outlook and a rich culture.*

China and taught in Singapore's schools as one of the official languages.

Malay Singaporeans

Singapore's Malay population descends from immigrants from the Malay Peninsula and the islands that are now Indonesia. They are often considered the "native" population of Singapore because Malay people arrived before the Chinese and Indians. Malay culture is a very important part of Singapore life—the national language is Malay, and the national anthem is sung in Malay.

▼ *A group of people meet in a Muslim district of Singapore. The women are wearing* tudung, *traditional Islamic scarves that cover their heads.*

Peranakans: Small Population, Big Influence

Peranakans are people of mixed Chinese and Malay descent (also known as Straits Chinese). The Peranakans originated in Malacca in the eighteenth century, when Chinese merchants settled and married local Malay women. As Singapore grew in importance, Peranakans settled in the city. Many were wealthy traders who built large mansions in the Emerald Hill and Katong districts of Singapore, becoming famous for their taste for sophisticated architecture and furnishings. Today, Peranakan culture is still a strong influence in Singapore, although only a tiny proportion of Singapore's population is Peranakan.

▲ *A woman prays at the Thian Hock Keng Temple.*
Built in 1842, it is Singapore's oldest Chinese temple.

Indian Singaporeans

Indian traders have long visited Singapore, but when Raffles landed in 1819, he brought with him more than one hundred sepoys, or soldiers, of the East India Company. These people formed the beginning of Singapore's Indian community. Singaporean

Indians originally came from all over India and Sri Lanka. Tamils, who come from southeastern India and northern Sri Lanka, make up about two-thirds of Singapore's Indian population. Tamil is an official language in Singapore, but many other Indian languages are spoken by other groups, including Malayalee, Punjabi, Bengali, and Telugu.

Religion

Not surprisingly in such a multi-ethnic society, there are a wide variety of religions in Singapore. All religions are practiced freely, as long as they do not conflict with state policy or racial harmony. The faith with the largest number of followers is Buddhism (42 percent of the population), followed by Islam (15 percent), Christianity (14 percent), Taoism (9 percent), and Hinduism (4 percent). Less than 1 percent follows other religions, and nearly 15 percent observe no religion.

In Singapore, religion is largely divided along ethnic lines. The Chinese population primarily follows the Buddhist and Taoist religions, while the Malay population is almost all Muslim. The Indian population includes Hindus (more than half of the Indian population), Muslims (nearly one-quarter), Christians, and Sikhs. Most Eurasians are Christian. However, Christians in Singapore come from all ethnic backgrounds, and in recent years, many younger Chinese Singaporeans have been turning to Christianity. Built in

1835, the oldest Christian church in Singapore is the Armenian Church of St. Gregory. There is also an Anglican cathedral, St. Andrew's, and the Roman Catholic Cathedral of the Good Shepherd, both Christian churches built in the nineteenth century. Many other minority religions are also followed in Singapore, such as Jainism, Zoroastrianism, and Mormonism.

Chinese Beliefs

Most Chinese Singaporeans combine a mixture of religions that includes Buddhism and Taoism, as well as elements of Confucianism. Buddhism is based on the teachings of Siddhartha Gautama who lived in Nepal in about the fifth century B.C. He became known as the Buddha, the "enlightened one." Taoism is a native Chinese religion, founded by Lao-tzu in the sixth century B.C. A philosophy rather than a religion, Confucianism is based on the teachings of Confucius, the Latin name of K'ung Fu-tzu, who lived in China in about the fifth century B.C.

Chinese Singaporeans worship in temples that include some of the oldest buildings to survive on the island. Thian Hock Keng Temple, built in 1839, stands in Chinatown. Dedicated to the goddess of the sea, it is of special significance to the Hokkien community, who were traditionally seafarers. The Kong Meng San Phor Kark See Temple is one of the largest Buddhist centers in southeast Asia.

Islam

Islam means "submission to Allah," or God. The Muslim faith began in Arabia in the seventh century A.D. and was brought to Southeast Asia by Muslim merchants from Yemen and India. The Muslim faith shapes the lives of the Malay population in Singapore, with Friday prayers at the many mosques on the island and fasting during Ramadan, the ninth month of the Islamic calendar. With a prayer hall that can hold up to five thousand worshipers, the Sultan Mosque is the main mosque in Singapore.

▼ *Brightly colored statues adorn the spectacular entrance to the Sri Mariamman Hindu temple.*

It is in Kampong Glam, the main community for Malay and Muslim Singaporeans.

Hinduism

A set of beliefs that developed over thousands of years in India, Hinduism emphasizes the right way to live. Hindus believe that life is a series of rebirths and that the results of a person's actions in one life are carried over into the next life. Hindus worship many different gods and goddesses. The oldest Hindu temple in Singapore, Sri Mariamman, is dedicated to the three main deities, Brahma, Vishnu, and Shiva, as well as the goddess Sri Mariamman.

▲ *Fireworks light up the sky while a parade takes place in Singapore's National Stadium as part of the National Day celebrations.*

Festivals

With its mix of people and religions, Singapore holds festivals and special days nearly all year round. Many of the religious festivals are based on the lunar calendar so their dates change from year to year. However, one festival that always occurs on the same date is Singapore's National Day on August 9, when all of Singapore celebrates the country's independence, declared in 1965. Marked by a parade of bands, acrobats, and dancers at either the National Stadium or on the Padang (a playing field in the center of Singapore), National Day finishes with a spectacular laser and fireworks display.

The Chinese Year

The most important festival for the Chinese community in Singapore is Chinese New Year in January or February. Chinatown is decorated in red, the color of good luck. Dragon and lion dancers perform in the streets to keep away the bad monsters associated with New Year. Across Singapore, shops and businesses close, and families get together to celebrate the New Year.

There are many other Chinese festivals. Families visit the temples and graves of their ancestors to give offerings of food and incense during Qing Ming, held in the spring. The Dragon Boat Festival in June is an international event, attracting teams from all over the world to race colorful dragon boats across Marina Bay. The Festival of the Hungry Ghosts in August or September is a time when Taoists believe that the spirits of the dead wander the earth. During this festival, street performers relate the stories of favorite Chinese legends in performances of Chinese opera. The Mid-Autumn Festival (sometimes known as the Moon Cake Festival), usually in October, is marked with parades of lanterns and special mooncakes, which are small, sweet pastries.

The most important celebration for Buddhists is Vesak in May or June, when they honor the life of the Buddha. Celebrations are held in Buddhist temples across Singapore, and caged birds are set free to symbolize the soul's release.

Muslim Celebrations

The main festivals for Muslims in Singapore are Hari Raya Puasa and Hari Raya Haji. Both can fall at any time of the year, depending on the Muslim calendar. Hari Raya Puasa marks the end of Ramadan, the Islamic holy month when Muslims fast from dawn until sunset. People go to the Geylang and Joo Chiat areas to buy special food associated with the festival, including *ketupat*, a type of rice cake. Hari Raya Haji is held to celebrate those who have made the hajj, the Muslim pilgrimage to Mecca in Saudi Arabia.

Hindu Festivals

The most important date in the Hindu calendar is Deepavali (or Diwali) in October or November, the festival of lights. Indian families put lights outside their homes, and Hindu temples are lit with thousands of colorful lights. People visit temples and shrines to make offerings. Two spectacular Indian festivals are Thaipusam in January or February and Thimithi in October or November. During Thaipusam, devotees of the Hindu god Lord Subramaniam walk about 2 miles (3 km) from Sri Srinivasa Perumal Temple to Sri Thandayuthapani using metal spikes pushed through their skin to carry colorfully

Pilgrimage to Kusu Island

Every year, many Singaporeans make a pilgrimage to Kusu Island, south of the main island of Singapore. There, Chinese Taoists make offerings at Tua Pek Kong Temple, while Muslims visit a Malay shrine. This is to honor a legend that recounts how a turtle turned itself into an island to save two shipwrecked sailors, one Malay and one Chinese.

decorated metal shrines. Thimithi is a Tamil fire-walking festival, held at the Sri Mariamman Temple. Devotees walk across red-hot coals without any apparent injury.

Food

Because of Singapore's ethnic diversity, there is a huge range of cuisines and an enormous choice of places to eat them, stretching from food stalls at hawker centers (large food centers) to world-class restaurants. Singaporeans can buy fresh food from markets such as the Tekka Centre, the Chinatown Complex, or Geylang Serai, where meat, fresh fish and seafood, and a wide range of fresh vegetables, herbs, and spices are offered.

Singapore has its own unique cuisine—the food of the Peranakan people, which is a blend of Chinese and Malay cooking. Traditionally, the best Peranakan cooking has been prepared in private homes because of the length of time it takes to make the food, but in recent times there has been a revival of interest in Peranakan cooking in Singapore's restaurants. The basis of Peranakan cuisine is the *rempah*, a blend of spices such as galangal, turmeric, and ginger with ingredients such as shallots, shrimp paste, and chilies. These are ground with a stone pestle and mortar called a *batu tumbok*. Typical Peranakan dishes include *ark tim* (sour duck soup), *otak otak* (barbecued curry fish), and *chicken kurmah* (chicken cooked with spicy prawn paste).

Chinese Food

Different regions of China have very different traditions of cooking, and Singapore contains many of them. Often, the type of cooking reflects the background and history of their origin. Dishes from the capital of China, Beijing, can be very elaborate, based on an ancient tradition of preparing banquets for the emperor's court, while the cooking of the rural Hakka people is frugal and simple, often using animal parts such as brains and feet. The most popular Chinese cuisines in Singapore are the fiery flavors of Sichuan cooking and Cantonese, with its fresh ingredients and light sauces. Although the Hokkien people make up the majority of the Chinese Singaporean population, Hokkien cuisine is not so well known. Some, however, consider Hokkien *mee*, which is egg noodles with pork, squid, prawns, and vegetables, the national dish of Singapore.

Indian and Malay Cuisines

Religion is an important factor in Indian and Malay cuisine: Muslims eat no pork while

Hindus eat no beef. Many Buddhists are vegetarians or vegans, who eat no eggs or dairy products. Traditions of Indian cuisine vary between southern India, where the food is often quite spicy, and northern India, where the food tends to be milder and creamier. Restaurants on Serangoon Road in Singapore serve southern Indian food on banana leaves. This food is scooped up and eaten with the fingers.

Malay cooking uses a wide array of spices such as coriander, tamarind, lime leaves, and lemongrass. One of the best-known Malay dishes in Singapore is satay, skewers of chicken, beef, or lamb that have been marinated in spices and then barbecued over hot charcoal.

◄ *This cook works quickly at a food stall in Chinatown. These stalls, known as hawker stalls, provide inexpensive food that is prepared while you wait.*

Forbidden Fruit: The Stinky Durian

A fruit grown in Southeast Asia, the durian has a prickly, hard outer casing that can be split open to reveal a soft yellow fruit. The durian season in Singapore runs from June to December, and Singaporeans love to eat these large fruits, which are usually about 10 inches (25 centimeters) long. The durian has a very strong smell—so strong and so unacceptable to some people that many hotels have banned durians altogether on their premises.

CHAPTER 3

Living in Singapore

Singapore has built its success on a strong Singaporean identity that incorporates elements of Western society with the Asian roots of the Singaporean population. The creation of this identity has helped to bind together the Chinese, Malay, and Indian populations into a single nation.

The core values at the center of the Singaporean identity are family and community, deference to authority, racial tolerance, agreement, order, and discipline. The idea that loyalty to family and community is more important than individual freedom is deeply rooted in many Asian cultures. This idea is balanced in the Singaporean identity by respect for the individual and by acknowledgment of individual achievements; Singaporean society respects and rewards people who work hard and show talent.

Government Campaigns

Ever since independence, the Singaporean government has actively tried to promote a Singaporean identity and influence how people behave through government campaigns and legislation. These numerous campaigns range from encouraging people to smile to keeping the streets of Singapore clean. Some people think that the millions of dollars spent on these campaigns is

◄ *Singapore's clean streets, such as this one at the Boat Quay, prove that its strict antilittering laws work.*

worthwhile because they benefit society as a whole. Others are more skeptical about their effects and voice fears about the government having too much control over Singaporean society.

After independence, the new nation faced a lack of both housing and jobs, so one of the earliest campaigns encouraged parents to limit the number of children in a family to two. Over the last two decades, however, birth rates have dropped, and Singapore's government faces the opposite problem—not enough people to fuel its ever-expanding economy. Now posters around the city encourage families to "Have three, more if you can afford it."

Other campaigns have included the "Keep Singapore Clean Campaign," the "Courtesy Campaign" to encourage people to be polite to each other, the "Smile

▲ *Singapore's Courtesy Campaign is designed to encourage citizens to show kindness and understanding toward each other and toward visitors.*

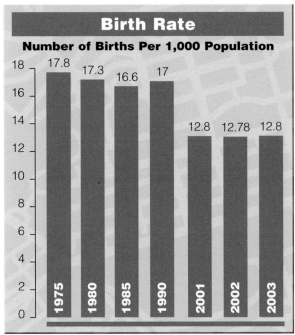

Birth Rate

Number of Births Per 1,000 Population

Year	Births per 1,000
1975	17.8
1980	17.3
1985	16.6
1990	17
2001	12.8
2002	12.78
2003	12.8

Source: United Nations Monthly Bulletin of Statistics and U.S. Census Bureau

Difficult Issues

Despite the strong promotion of the Singaporean identity, some difficult issues between the three populations in Singapore remain. A large proportion of Singapore's population is Chinese, and some people fear that Chinese voices are too influential in government and business. In recent years, many young and well-educated Indians have emigrated from Singapore, mostly to Australia, Canada, and the United States; some blame job market discrimination that favors the Chinese Singaporeans for many Indians' decision to leave. The Malay population also has its problems, with the highest proportion of drug addicts in the country and high crime statistics. Historically, the Malays have been farmers, not business people, which has led them to take poorly paid jobs in commerce-oriented Singapore.

▲ *The majority of Singaporeans live in Housing and Development Board apartment buildings.*

Singapore Campaign" to encourage people to smile at each other, and the "Speak Mandarin Campaign." Laws also control smoking, gum chewing, and flushing public toilets after use. A controversial law passed in 1996 is designed to make people take care of their elderly parents.

Housing Problems and Solutions

When Singapore became independent, many people on the island were living in slums and squatter settlements. Earlier in the twentieth century, the colonial government had attempted to improve conditions and built some new housing. World War II, however, interrupted these attempts. After the war, plans were drawn up to build more housing, but no construction work ever started. By 1965, Singapore was mainly a city of slum developments. In the drive to improve housing conditions and encourage economic growth, bulldozers destroyed whole neighborhoods to make way for new developments; there was little time for concern about historic buildings.

The urgent need for more housing led the government to establish the Housing and Development Board (HDB) in 1960. Today, over 80 percent of Singaporeans live in high-rise, government-built apartment blocks, most located away from the center of Singapore in twenty-one "new towns." These new towns have been carefully planned to offer residents all the facilities they need, for example shops, schools, libraries, parks, sports centers, and movie theaters. A good public transportation system links the new towns to the center of Singapore and to each other.

In the early days of the HDB, the government needed to construct apartment blocks quickly and kept designs simple to ensure speedy construction. Since the 1980s, however, architects have designed the apartment blocks with more imagination to satisfy the higher expectations of residents. There are also new projects such as Punggol 21 on the coast in northeast Singapore. At Punggol 21, there is a mixture of 60 percent government-built public housing, 30 $1/4\%$ private housing, and 10 percent luxurious executive condominiums.

Preserving the Nation's Heritage

It was not until the 1970s and 1980s that efforts began to preserve some of the historical areas and buildings of old Singapore. In 1981, the Urban Redevelopment Authority (URA) and other official organizations declared the Peranakan neighborhood on Emerald Hill Road to be the first area to be given conservation status. They hoped to preserve the elaborate facades (outside fronts) of more than one hundred houses and shophouses (stores with homes above the retail space). In 1988, Chinatown (pictured below), Little India, Boat Quay and Kampung Glam also became official conservation areas. Today, more than sixty such areas in Singapore cover more than six thousand buildings.

▲ Both Singaporeans and tourists flock to the malls on Orchard Road, Singapore's most fashionable shopping area.

Rising Prices

Despite its huge investment in public housing, Singapore faces some of the most expensive property prices in the world. Rising prices have affected both private and public housing, making it very difficult for many first-time buyers to afford a home. Most families must rely on two incomes to afford an HDB apartment.

Striking a Bargain

Stores in Singapore range from huge malls and mega-stores to neighborhood shops in the new towns that provide for local shoppers' needs. Because the Singapore dollar can't buy as much as it used to and inflation is rising, prices of goods in Singapore are no longer as cheap as they once were. Many Singaporeans head abroad to Bangkok, Kuala Lumpur, or Jakarta to find real bargains. Singapore remains a shopping paradise, however, with most stores open from 10 A.M. until 9 P.M. daily.

While some shops such as department stores and supermarkets have fixed prices, bargaining is normal in most other situations. Most Singaporean shoppers will always have an idea of the average price of the goods they want to buy and will try to reduce the asking price of an item by polite negotiation with the shopkeeper. Most of the time, they end up paying between 60 percent and 80 percent of the first asking price.

Orchard and Serangoon Roads

Once lined with orchards and plantations of nutmeg trees, the main shopping street in central Singapore is Orchard Road, a wide, tree-lined avenue that stretches 1.5 miles (2.5 km). Huge shopping malls, each one trying to outdo the others, line the road. The largest is Ngee Ann City, which houses some of the most prestigious and expensive retailers in the world. While many Singaporeans love to window-shop in such places, they are more likely to spend money

"To Make Singapore a Great City to Live, Work and Play"

—Slogan of the Urban Development Authority.

at the Centrepoint Shopping Centre, which has less expensive shops such as Robinsons department store.

Smaller shops have survived in Singapore, but redevelopment has often meant that these stores have been moved from their traditional shophouses into large complexes. This is what happened in Chinatown, where thousands of shophouses were demolished, and their businesses rehoused in centers such

Singapore Shophouses

A shophouse is exactly what the name implies— a store with living quarters attached, usually on the upper floor. Raffles started shophouse design in Singapore, but shophouses are also found in the other places that were part of the British Straits Settlements (Malacca and Penang). There are five different periods of Singaporean shophouse, each with its own type of design and decoration. Many have been demolished over the years, but since the 1970s, the government has acted to preserve and restore some of the survivors, like these pictured above. Today, shophouses are highly prized for their architectural heritage.

as the Chinatown Complex. Small stores have survived in their original settings, however, in Serangoon Road in Little India. Here, people go to buy Indian spices, jewelry, and clothes and eat delicious Indian food at the many restaurants lining the road.

Education

Education in Singapore is tightly linked to the creation of a Singaporean identity. As well as teaching children the usual subjects, school is seen as a place where children should learn to "love and know Singapore" and "to look into the principles by which Singapore is led and governed."

The school year consists of four ten-week terms beginning on January 2 each year with a one-week vacation after the first and third term, a four-week vacation in the middle of the year, and six weeks off at the end of the year. Children are taught in English as a first language and in Chinese, Malay, or Tamil as their native language. Many schools offer all three native languages, but some offer only one, for example, teaching in English and Chinese only.

Primary Education

Kindergartens exist for children age three to six, but compulsory (required) education starts with primary school at the age of six. Primary education is divided into two parts, a four-year foundation stage and a two-year orientation stage. Foundation-stage teachers strive to give children a firm grounding in English as well as their native tongue and

mathematics. Students also study other subjects such as music, art, morals, and health. At the end of this stage, children are divided into three different ability groups. The top two groups continue to study English and their native language, as well as mathematics and science. The lower group takes more basic language and mathematics instruction. At the end of primary school, pupils take the Primary School Leaving Examination (PSLE) to assess their abilities for secondary school.

Secondary and Junior Colleges

There are three types of secondary education—Normal, Special, and Express. Those taking the Normal course can choose between academic and vocational options. The Special course is for pupils who are strong in both English and their native language and have come within the top 10 percent in the PSLE. In this course, pupils continue to study languages as well as the humanities (for example, history and geography), mathematics, and science. The Express course is similar, but suits those who are not so strong in English and their native language. Both lead students to the General Certificate of Education (GCE) Ordinary level exams after they complete four years of study.

The Special and Express courses prepare pupils for pre-university courses at junior colleges and universities, while students following Normal courses often go on to attend vocational courses at Singapore's

▲ *Students at a Singapore school check their temperature with guidance from their teacher. These exercises are part of the Ministry of Education's plan to combat disease and encourage people to take responsibility for their own health.*

polytechnic colleges. The fifteen junior colleges in Singapore are designed to give students more independence than they had at secondary school. Students work toward GCE Advanced level exams necessary to attend a university.

Higher Education

Singapore contains three universities—the National University of Singapore, the Nanyang Technological University, and the Singapore Management University. The first two are public universities, while the Singapore Management University is

"An educated person is also someone who is responsible to his community and country."

—From Singapore Ministry of Education Web site describing the desired outcome of education.

privately run, although funded by the government, and offers a broad-based business curriculum.

Getting There and Getting Around

Singapore's large and busy ports provide primarily for commercial ships, although some cruise ships dock at HarbourFront Centre on Singapore's southern coast. From here, ferries leave for and arrive from destinations such as Sentosa and Batan and the Bintan Islands in the Riau Archipelago. For many people, however, the easiest way to travel into and out of Singapore is by plane. Singapore's international airport, Changi, is the busiest air hub in the region, handling more than fifty different airlines and more than 24 million passengers a year.

Those who need to reach the Malay Peninsula north of Singapore travel by car, bus, or on the train. Drivers must pay tolls to use the two road links bridging Singapore and Malaysia. The older of the two links, the Woodlands Causeway, often gets very congested, but the link at Tuas farther west is less heavily used. Trains run daily between Singapore and Kuala Lumpur, and it is possible to catch connections to travel to Bangkok in Thailand.

For traveling around the island, Singapore offers an excellent, clean, efficient public transportation service. Public transportation is crucial; the government taxes cars so heavily that many people do not have one. Singapore's Mass Rapid Transit (MRT) System opened in

▶ MRT trains run underground in and around Singapore's downtown area, but most of the track is either at street level or elevated.

1987 and goes both under and above ground. Its three main lines link the four corners of the island with the center. A Light Rapid Transit System also connects the new towns east of Choa Chu Kang in the center of the island to the MRT line. Buses are cheaper than the MRT and are also extremely efficient. Nonair-conditioned buses cost slightly less than air-conditioned ones.

To reduce traffic congestion and pollution, the government actively discourages Singaporeans from owning a car. To buy a car or motorbike, the purchaser

The City without Traffic Jams

Singapore is one of the few major cities in the world that does not suffer from traffic problems—partly because of the measures taken to control car ownership. The government also strictly controls traffic during rush hours. As of the mid-1970s, central Singapore has been a restricted zone for traffic. Until recently, drivers who wanted to bring their vehicles into the area between the hours of 7.30 A.M. and 6.30 P.M. had to buy a special permit. Now, an Electronic Road Pricing system has replaced this method with a computerized card that automatically charges drivers for using certain stretches of road and restricted zones.

must have a Certificate of Entitlement (CEO), which is valid for ten years. The government sells CEOs and tightly controls the number on the market. Even once the buyer has obtained a CEO, he or she has to pay some of the highest prices in the world for a new car, thanks to taxes imposed by the government. Fuel is also heavily taxed, and the annual road tax is also very expensive. Nevertheless, 32 percent of Singaporeans own cars, although only one-quarter of the population uses a car to commute to work.

CHAPTER 4

Singapore at Work

Singapore's economic miracle since independence has been built on its unique location, strong government, political stability, and the creation of an excellent infrastructure, such as its efficient transportation system. Much of this achievement has been due to the vision of Singapore's prime minister for thirty-one years, Lee Kuan Yew. Singapore's bad reputation for strikes and worker unrest once discouraged companies from building factories there. Under Yew's leadership, however, relations between workers and employers improved. In exchange for stricter working practices negotiated with the unions, the government promised improved housing and cheap and efficient public transportation. Lee Kuan Yew also reduced Singapore's traditional reliance on trade with Great Britain, with its smaller number of businesses, and started work to increase trade with industrial giants such as the United States and large multinational companies. These policies were so successful that by the 1970s, Singapore had full employment and a booming economy.

Manufacturing

In the early years of independence, Singapore's economy relied on manufacturing

◄ *Singapore's main island has one of the largest and busiest ports in the world.*

High-Tech City

Computer technology is used throughout Singapore to ensure that the nation runs smoothly. For example, computers control and monitor Singapore's transportation systems. Since 2002, travelers pay by using computerized cards that automatically charge the correct amount for any journey. Keeping at the forefront of high-tech developments is very important for Singapore, and the government is investing heavily in education and technology for the future.

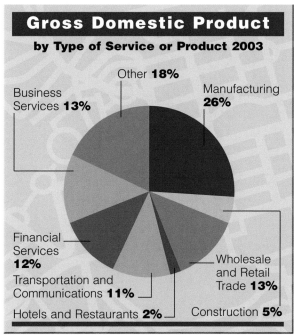

Gross Domestic Product
by Type of Service or Product 2003

Other **18%**
Business Services **13%**
Manufacturing **26%**
Financial Services **12%**
Transportation and Communications **11%**
Hotels and Restaurants **2%**
Wholesale and Retail Trade **13%**
Construction **5%**

Manpower Research and Statistics Department

▲ *Gross Domestic Product (GDP) is the total value of all the goods and services produced in a region during a particular period of time, usually one year.*

products for export. The main products included textiles and clothes, transportation equipment, and petroleum products. The government worked to improve the education of the workforce and to attract companies that needed highly skilled workers who could operate complex machinery. As a result, multinational companies such as Sony and Matsushita began to invest in Singapore and to set up manufacturing plants. During the 1970s and 1980s, manufacturing complex electrical equipment became increasingly important. By the late 1980s, Singapore produced at least half of all the disk drives used to power the world's computers.

Another vital element in Singapore's economy was petroleum. By the late 1980s, Singapore was the world's third largest petroleum-refining and oil-trading center. Singaporeans also built oil-drilling rigs and

repaired and maintained oil rigs and tankers. Supported by demand from China's growing economy, oil refining and ship and rig maintenance are still an important part of the economy.

Close ties to multinational companies become a disadvantage, however, when other countries go into recession. For example, if a country such as Japan experiences an economic downturn and people buy fewer computers, it directly impacts the Singaporean manufacturing industry. For this reason, Singapore's government has helped to establish small, local businesses that are involved in a wide

range of activities including shipbuilding, processing food, and manufacturing plastics, paper products, electrical products, and transportation equipment.

Finance and Business

Since the late 1970s, Singapore's government has also encouraged developing finance and business activities. These categories include jobs such as accounting, advertising, legal work, banking, management consulting, architecture, telecommunications, and engineering. By the 1990s, Singapore had become the fourth biggest center for trading in the major world currencies such as the U.S. dollar, the Japanese yen, and the Euro.

The heart of Singapore's financial district runs along the waterfront south of the Singapore River. Its two main roads are Shenton Way and Robinson Road; Raffles Place is the main hub of commercial life in Singapore. The whole area is full of skyscrapers housing the world's biggest financial and commercial institutions. Many of the most notable were designed by foreign architects, including the Chinese-American I. M. Pei, who built the OCBC Centre and others, and the Japanese architect Kenzo Tange, who designed the OUB Building in Raffles Place.

◄ City workers walk in front of a stock exchange information board displaying share prices in Raffles Place, Singapore's financial center.

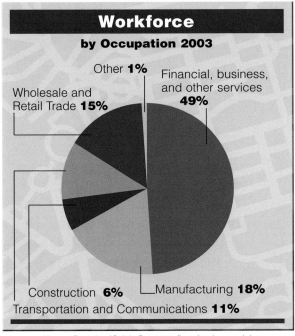

Workforce
by Occupation 2003

Other **1%**

Financial, business, and other services **49%**

Wholesale and Retail Trade **15%**

Construction **6%**

Manufacturing **18%**

Transportation and Communications **11%**

Manpower Research and Statistics Department – figures have been rounded

Singapore's Workforce

Like many other aspects of life in Singapore, the workforce has traditionally been divided along ethnic lines. The Hokkiens have been most economically successful among Chinese Singaporeans, dominating banking, financial services, insurance, and real estate. The next largest group in the Chinese community, the Teochews largely continue their traditional occupations working in the fresh-produce trade, fishing, and running jewelry businesses. The Cantonese are associated with the restaurant trade, while the Hakkas and Hainanese are found mostly in manual trades and the domestic-service industries.

Singapore's Indian population came from many different parts of India and Sri Lanka and is often grouped together according to their traditional occupations. Today, the Chettiars, wealthy moneylenders from Madras, still work in Chulia, Market, and Malacca Streets around the financial heart of Singapore. From northern India, Sikhs, Sindhis, and Gujaratis have businesses along High Street in the old colonial quarter north of Singapore River selling textiles and electronic goods.

While these traditional divisions continue in the twenty-first century, Singapore provides a wealth of great opportunity for most of its citizens. In fact, one of Singapore's problems for the future is its need for highly qualified engineers and scientists to keep its industries at the cutting edge of world development. To find such highly qualified people, the Singapore Economic Development Board (EDB) recruits thousands of workers every year from areas such as India and Eastern Europe.

A Nation of Savers

Singapore's laws require all working citizens to save a large proportion of their income. About 20 percent of a person's monthly salary (the amount is recalculated each year) goes directly into the Central Provident Fund (CPF). People are permitted to use some of this money to pay for a mortgage (loan) to buy HDB apartments. Some of it is used for medical insurance, and some of it provides a pension for old age. Employers have to match their employee's contribution into the CPF.

Singapore's Government

Singapore is a republic with a parliamentary system of government modeled on the British parliamentary system. The government is made up of three parts: the executive (the Cabinet), the legislature (Parliament), and the judiciary (the Supreme Court and other courts).

The president is the head of state. Before 1991, Parliament appointed the president and his role was mainly ceremonial; he held little real power. (As of 2004, there have been no female presidents.) In 1991, the constitution of the Republic of Singapore was amended to change the way the president was appointed and the president's duties. The amendments allowed for all citizens of Singapore to vote for their president, who would then serve for a fixed term of six years. The amended constitution also gave the president power to challenge and question government policy in some areas. In 1993, Ong Teng Cheong became the first elected president; S. R. Nathan was elected in 1999. A group called the Council of Presidential Advisers assists the president.

The Parliament and Cabinet

The role of Parliament is to make laws, to control the state's finances, and to question the policies and actions of the governing party. Before a law can be passed, it must be introduced in Parliament as a draft called a bill. All bills are then debated in Parliament and are often amended before they can become law. The president must approve all bills.

The Singapore Parliament is modeled on the British system of parliamentary democracy. At least every five years, all Singapore citizens vote to elect the members of Parliament in general elections. The main political party in Singapore is the People's Action Party (PAP), and in the 2001 elections, they won 75 percent of the vote, producing eighty-two out of eighty-four members of Parliament. The leading opposition parties are the Workers' Party (one member of Parliament), the Singapore Democratic Party (one member of Parliament), the Singapore Democratic Alliance, and the Democratic Progressive Party.

The president asks the leader of the political party that wins a general election to become the prime minister (PM), the most powerful person in Singapore's politics. The PM then selects the cabinet from the elected members of Parliament and leads it. Since the cabinet is responsible for all government policies and the administration of affairs of the state, the cabinet is very powerful. For thirty-one years (from 1959 to 1990), Lee Kuan Yew was prime minister of Singapore. He stepped down in 1990, and Goh Chok Tong took his place. Lee Kuan Yew remains a powerful figure in Singapore's government, however, since he is the senior minister in Goh Chok Tong's cabinet.

Parliament House

Until 1999, Parliament was housed in an old mansion that was built between 1826 and 1827. It stands on Parliament Lane near the site where Raffles first landed in Singapore in 1819. In 1999, however, Parliament moved into a new Parliament House because the old building was too small. The new Parliament House (pictured below) is a low-rise building that combines elements of modern and traditional styles.

CHAPTER 5

Singapore at Play

Singapore has a vibrant cultural scene, with plays, concerts, dance, films, and art exhibitions. Many international touring companies come to Singapore, performing at venues such as the Victoria Theatre and Concert Hall or the Kallang Theatre. In 2002, a new performing arts center called The Esplanade—Theatres on the Bay opened on Singapore's waterfront with the aim of making Singapore the main arts center for the whole region.

The Music Scene

In its early years as an independent nation, the government's drive for economic development left little time to nurture the local arts scene. In recent decades, however, Singapore's government has recognized the importance of the arts, and in 1991, it set up the National Arts Council and created a government Ministry for the Arts. Founded in 1979, the Singapore Symphony Orchestra has its home in the Victoria Concert Hall, where the orchestra performs the classics of Western symphony repertoire as well as special commissions from local Asian composers. The Singapore Chinese Orchestra was founded in 1996 and plays at

◄ *Elaborate costumes and make up are combined with song, mime, and dance in Chinese opera, a traditional Chinese form of theater that is regularly performed in Singapore's Chinatown area.*

► *Esplanade—Theatres on the Bay (in foreground) is a spectacular arts complex built on reclaimed land on Singapore's waterfront. It contains a concert hall, theater, two studios, and outdoor performing spaces.*

the Singapore Conference Hall. Malay and Indian orchestras also perform regularly.

International popular singers often include dates in Singapore as part of a world tour, usually performing at the Singapore Indoor Stadium or at the Esplanade—Theatres on the Bay where the largest concert hall holds eighteen hundred people. Acts in Western and Cantopop (a style of pop music written in Cantonese and originating in Hong Kong in the late 1970s) music are both very popular. World-music fans enjoy the World of Music, Art and Dance (WOMAD) festival, held for four days every year in Fort Canning Park.

Museums

From stamps at the Singapore Philatelic Museum to bugs at the Insect Kingdom Museum on Sentosa Island, Singapore's museums satisfy a wide range of interests. Some museums cover Singapore's history, for example, the Singapore History Museum; the Malay Village, a showcase for Malay arts and crafts; and the Changi Chapel and Museum, a replica of a Japanese prisoner-of-war camp that once stood in Singapore. For art lovers, the Singapore Art Museum, which opened in 1996, is a showcase for over four thousand pieces of Southeast Asian art. It also hosts traveling exhibitions from all over the world.

Theater and Movies

Singapore has a wide variety of theater companies, ranging from Act Three, which specializes in children's theater, to Teater Kami, which often stages controversial plays in the Malay language. The Singapore Repertory Theatre performs English-language plays at the DBS Arts Centre. Musicals are very popular in Singapore, and international hits such as Andrew Lloyd Webber's *Cats* and *Miss Saigon* have been huge box-office draws. Called *Chang and Eng*, a local musical about conjoined twins was also a huge success and has since toured all over Asia.

Going to the movies is a major recreational activity for Singaporeans, with many people going to see a film two or even three times a week, usually at theaters in shopping centers. The most popular films are Hollywood blockbusters, Indian movies made in Bombay, and Hong Kong action movies. Films are shown in English with Chinese subtitles. If a film is in another language, it usually has both English and Chinese subtitles. An International Film Festival is held every year in April or May for two weeks.

Sports

One of the Singaporean government's social campaigns encouraged its citizens to have a healthy lifestyle. In support of this, the Ministry of Education launched the Trim and Fit Programme in 1992 to improve fitness among school-age children. Today, many people in Singapore exercise regularly, and sports such as running, biking, and walking are increasingly popular. Miles of jogging and biking paths cover the island. Popular spots include the Botanic Gardens in central Singapore; East Coast Park, where paths take runners along the edge of the Singapore Strait; and the parks of the Central Catchment Nature Reserve. Singapore plans to link parks and nature reserves with "green corridors" over the next thirty years.

Many Singaporeans like to play golf, and there are at least eighteen golf courses. Bowling, badminton, and tennis are also

"Vision—

To develop Singapore as a distinctive global city for the arts"

"Mission—

To nurture the arts and make it an integral part of the lives of the people of Singapore"

—Slogans of the Singapore National Arts Council.

very popular. Not surprisingly given Singapore's location and climate, water sports are a major recreational activity. There are several diving clubs and sailing schools, as well as opportunities to canoe, windsurf, water ski, and wakeboard, in which a motorboat pulls a person on top of a buoyant board in the wake behind the boat. Sentosa Island and East Coast Park

Two Nature Reserves

In the center of the island of Singapore lies a large, green expanse called the Central Catchment Nature Reserve made up of three parks—the MacRitchie Reservoir Park, Pierce Reservoir Park, and Seletar Reservoir Park. It is one of only two nature reserves in Singapore, the other being Bukit Timah, just to the west. This area allows a glimpse into what Singapore was like before the land was cleared and built on. It also provides a vital resource for Singaporeans who want to escape from the city and walk through beautiful green surroundings.

are favorite destinations for water sports of all kinds.

One of the most popular spectator sports is horseracing. During the racing season, people flock to the Singapore Turf Club to watch races such as the Raffles Cup and the Singapore Cup, which commemorates the first race run in 1843. Fans can watch Singapore's national soccer team in action at

▲ *People play volleyball at Siloso Beach, Sentoso Island. With parkland, gardens, nature walks, museums, hotels, restaurants, and three beaches, Sentosa is one of Singapore's main tourist attractions.*

the National Stadium. Another reminder of British colonial days comes with games of cricket at the Padang and polo matches played at the Singapore Polo Club.

CHAPTER 6

Looking Forward

"Water is a scarce commodity in Singapore. We have to curb the upward trend in consumption of water, and make its prudent use an ingrained habit. If not, we will be short of water in fifteen to twenty years' time. We have to take water conservation measures now to slow down its increasing demand." These words of Prime Minister Goh Chok Tong underline one of the most difficult problems facing Singapore for the future. Singapore's only local source of water is rainfall collected in its fourteen reservoirs. The remainder of Singapore's water supplies comes from the south Malaysian state of Johor. The rising demand for water, however, means that supplies will soon start to run out.

The government is tackling the problem through a campaign to urge people to save water and by raising taxes on water consumption. It is also looking for new sources of water. One possibility is to import water from Indonesia. Another is to build desalination plants to turn seawater into freshwater. However, desalination uses large amounts of energy and is therefore very expensive. It seems certain that Singaporeans will have to use water

◀ *The thirty-seven-story office building of Centennial Tower was designed with Singapore's future needs in mind; it is possible to expand the building by a further fifteen stories.*

> *"… only through creativity and innovation can Singapore differentiate itself from other economies."*
>
> —National Science and Technology Board chairman Mr. Teo Ming Kian, 1998.

more carefully in the future and will have to pay more for the water they do use.

A United Nation Made of Many Peoples

In May 1999, Prime Minister Goh Chok Tong told Parliament that Singapore was not yet a nation and that it could take two or more generations before a successful, truly multiracial state was built. The ongoing challenge for Singaporeans is to forge a sense of nationhood in Singapore's multicultural and multiracial population.

One problem is that Singapore is often seen as a "Chinese nation," surrounded geographically by Malay- and Muslim-dominated states. After the terrorist attacks of September 11, 2001, in New York and Washington, D.C., Deputy Prime Minister Lee Hsien Loong, the eldest son of Lee Kuan Yew, was asked how he saw the attacks affecting relations between the Muslim and other communities in Singapore. He replied, "It will be a test of our social cohesion. We must do everything we can to strengthen racial harmony."

The other continual challenge for the people of Singapore is to keep the nation's world reputation as a leading economy. Singapore experienced difficulties in the late 1990s and again in 2001, when the economy slowed down and unemployment rose. The government quickly stepped in to revive business and the economy picked up again.

Singapore is investing heavily in new technology to keep its businesses at the cutting edge of world industries. A plan known as Technopreneurship Singapore is aimed at creating an environment where business innovation can flourish, and a hi-tech science-park development called the Science Hub is being built to provide an environment where business and technology can work side by side. The development will be completed in phases over the next fifteen to twenty years and is intended to attract local and foreign talent. As always, Singaporeans are working hard and planning carefully for their future success.

Terminal 3

Singapore's position as the main transportation hub for the region will be boosted in 2008 when a third terminal at Changi Airport reaches completion. This terminal will have the ability to handle another 20 million passengers a year, bringing the total capacity of Changi Airport to 64 million passengers by the year 2020. The new terminal will employ some state-of-the-art technology, including a rapid baggage-handling system, allowing luggage to be moved around the airport in underground tunnels at high speed.

43

Timeline

A.D. 100s Greek astronomer and geographer, Ptolemy, identifies a trading center called Sabara near modern-day Singapore.

200s Chinese sailors describe a place called Pu-Luo-Chung, that may be Singapore.

1295 Italian explorer Marco Polo possibly stops at Temasek, as the area was known by Malays.

1365 The first written reference to Temasek appears in Javanese court records.

c.1390 Iskandar from Palembang supposedly founds Singapore.

1511 Portuguese capture Malacca on west coast of Malaya.

1641 Dutch take control of Malacca and Indonesia.

1819 Thomas Raffles arrives in Singapore and signs a treaty for the British East India Company to establish a trading base on the island.

1824 An agreement between British and Dutch governments gives Great Britain Penang, Malacca, and Singapore, known as the British Straits Settlements.

1869 The Suez Canal opens in Egypt, leading to an increase in ships docking at Singapore.

1888 H. N. Ridley brings rubber seedlings to Malaya; rubber becomes a major export from Singapore.

1941 Japan invades Malaya.

1942 Singapore surrenders to the Japanese; Japanese occupation begins.

1945 Both World War II and the Japanese occupation of Singapore end.

1955 The People's Action Party (PAP) is founded.

1959 PAP wins a majority of seats in elections, and Lee Kuan Yew becomes first prime minister of Singapore.

1960 Singapore's government establishes the Housing and Development Board (HDB).

1963 Singapore, Sabah, and Sarawak merge with Malaya to form Federation of Malaysia.

1965 Singapore separates from the Federation of Malaysia and becomes independent.

1987 Singapore's Mass Rapid Transit (MRT) System opens.

1990 Lee Kuan Yew steps down as prime minister, replaced by Goh Chok Tong.

2001 PAP wins 75 percent of the vote in general elections.

2002 The Esplanade—Theatres on the Bay opens.

2004 Deputy Prime Minister, Lee Hsien Loong, takes over from Goh Chok Tong.

Glossary

Bengali a language spoken by people from Bangladesh and West Bengal in India.

British Straits Settlements the name given to Penang, Malacca, and Singapore in 1824; became a British Crown Colony in 1867.

Buddhism a world religion founded by Siddhartha Gautama (c. 563–c. 483 B.C.), known as the Buddha. Buddhists believe in rebirth and that people's deeds during one life influence their successive lives.

Cantonese describes people originally from Hong Kong and Guangzhou and the language they speak.

causeway a raised road across wet ground or water.

Communism a political belief system in which the state plans and controls the economy, and property is held in common.

condominiums buildings made up of separate apartments that are owned, not rented.

Confucianism a philosophy based on the teachings of Confucius, the Latin name of K'ung Fu-tse who lived in China in about 400 B.C. Confucian thought stresses the importance of family and social ties and respect for authority.

Eurasians people of mixed Asian and European descent.

Hainanese describes people from the island of Hainan, an island in the South China Sea.

Hakka a people and language originally from central China.

hawker centers large food centers in Singapore, with tables and chairs at which people may eat food chosen from a range of stalls.

Hinduism a religion of India with many gods and goddesses; Hindus believe that a person is reborn many times.

Hokkiens people from Fujian province in southern China.

inflation an increase in the level of prices.

infrastructure the system of public works, such as water, electricity, and roads, in a region.

Islam a major world religion that started in the seventh century in Arabia. Islam is practiced by Muslims who believe in submission to God and in Mohammad as the chief and last prophet of God.

Malayalee (Malayalam) a language spoken by people from southwestern India.

mangrove a tree or shrub with stiltlike roots and stems that form dense thickets along ocean shores.

Peranakan describes people of mixed Chinese and Malay descent (also known as Straits Chinese).

prawns edible crustaceans that look like large shrimp.

Punjabi a language spoken by people from the Punjab region in northwest India.

recession a time of extended decline in economic activity.

shophouse a shop in Singapore with living quarters attached, usually above the shop.

Sikhs people who believe in Sikhism, a religion founded by Guru Nanak in the sixteenth century in India. Sikhs believe in one invisible God, and their sacred text is the Adi Granth.

Tamil the people and language of southern India and Sri Lanka.

Taosim a Chinese religion. Tao means the "path." Its founder Lao-tzu is said to have lived during the sixth century B.C.

Telugu a language spoken by people from southeast India.

Teochews people who originally came from the Shantou region of Guangdong in China.

Further Information

Books

Baker, James Michael, and Junia Marion Baker. *Singapore (Counties of the World)*. Gareth Stevens Publishing, 2002.

Kummer, Patricia, *Singapore (Enchantment of the World)*. Scholastic Library Publishing, 2003.

Layton, Lesley, and Pang Guek Cheng. *Singapore (Cultures of the World)*. Benchmark Books, 2001.

Rau, Dana Meachen. *Singapore (Discovering Cultures)*. Benchmark Books, 2004.

Thomas, Matt. *Singapore (Countries: Faces and Places)*. Child's World, 2001.

Yong, Ju Lin, James Michael Baker, and Junia Marion Baker. *Welcome to Singapore (Welcome to My Country)*. Gareth Stevens Publishing, 2003.

Web Sites

http://www.makantime.com
Discover the many kinds of delicious food available in Singapore on its unofficial food Web site.

www.nparks.gov.sg
The National Parks Board Web site lets you explore Singapore's many parks and learn about plants.

www.odci.gov/cia/publications/factbook/geos/sn.html
Search this CIA World Factbook site for detailed information on Singapore's people, government, political issues, and more.

www.parliament.gov.sg
Learn about Singapore's Parliament, its members, and its legislation from its official Web site.

www.underwaterworld.com.sg/home.html
Take a virtual tour of Asia's largest tropical aquarium with its twenty-five hundred marine animals.

Index

Page numbers in **bold** indicate pictures.

Act Three, 39
air travel, 30, 43
Armenian Church of St. Gregory, 17

badminton, 40
Bencoolen, 9
birth rate, 23
Boat Quay, 25
Botanic Gardens, 40
bowling, 40
Britain and the British, 4, 9, 10, 12, 13, 32
British East India Company, 9, 10, 16
British Straits Settlements, 10, 12, 27
Buddhism, 16, 17
Bukit Timah, 5, 6, 40
buses, 30

Cantonese, 7, 14, 20, 35, 39
cars, 30, 31
Cathedral of the Good Shepherd, 17
causeways, 5, 30
Central Catchment Nature Reserve, 6, 40
Central Provident Fund (CPF), 35
Centrepoint Shopping Centre, 27
Certificate of Entitlement (CEO), 31
Changi Airport, 30, 43
Changi Chapel and Museum, 39
Changi Prison, 12
Chettiars, 35
China, 11
Chinatown, 5, 10, 17, 25, **25**, 27
Chinatown Complex, 28
Chinese opera, **38**
Chinese population, 4, 5, 10, 11, 13, 14, 16, 17, 20, 24, 35
Christianity, 16
City Hall, 5
climate, 6–7
Communism, 11
computer technology, 33
Confucianism, 17
conservation, 25, 27
cricket, 41
cruise ships, 30

DBS Arts Centre, 39
department stores, 26
durian, 21
Dutch, the, 9, 10

East Coast Park, 40
economy, 4, 13, 32, 43
education, 28–30
Electronic Road Pricing System, 30
Emerald Hill Road, 25
Esplanade—Theatres on the Bay, 38, 39, **39**
Eurasian population, 4, 14, 16

farming, 5, 11
Farquhar, Colonel William, 10
ferries, 30
festivals, 18–19
finance and business, 34
financial district, 5, 34
food, 20–21
food stalls, 20, **21**

Goh Chok Tong, 36, 42, 43
golf, 40
government, 36–37
government campaigns, 22–24
Gross Domestic Product (GDP), 33
Gujaratis, 35

Hainanese, 14, 35
Hakkas, 14, 20, 35
hawker centers, 20
Hinduism, 16, **17**, 18
Hokkiens, 14, 17, 20, 35
horseracing, 41
housing, 24, 26, 32
Housing and Development Board (HDB), 24, 25, 26

immigration, 10, 11
independence, 12, 13
Indian population, 4, 5, 10, 14, 16, 20, 23, 35
Indonesia, 9
Insect Kingdom Museum, 39
International Film Festival, 40
Islam, 6, 15, 16, 17, 18, 19, 20, 43

Jainism, 17
Japan, 12, 33, 34

Japanese occupation, 12, 39
Johor, 42

Kallang Theatre, 38
Kampong Glam, 5, 10, 18, 25
kampung, 6, 7
Kong Meng San Phor Kark, 17
Kusu Island, 6, 20

landfill, 5
languages and dialects, 7, 14, 15, 16
    Bengali, 16
    Cantonese, 7
    English, 7
    Hakka, 7
    Malay, 7, 15
    Malayalee, 16
    Mandarin Chinese, 7, 14, 15
    Punjabi, 16
    Singlish, 7
    Tamil, 7, 16, 28
    Telugu, 16
Lee Hsien Loong, 43
Lee Kuan Yew, 13, **13**, 32, 36, 43
Light Rapid Transit System, 30
Little India, 5, 10, 25, 27

Majapahit, 8
Malacca, 9, 10, 27
Malay population, 4, 5, 14, 15, 16, 17, 18, 20, 21, 24
Malay Village, 39
Malaya, 9, 13
Malaya, Federation of, 12
Malaysia, 5, 13, 42
Malaysia, Federation of, 13
malls, 26, **26**
mangrove swamps, 6
manufacturing, 32–33
markets, 20
Mass Rapid Transit System (MRT), 30, 31
Mormonism, 17
movies, 40
museums, 39, 41
music, 38–39
Muslim (*see* Islam)

Nathan, S.R., 36
National Arts Council, 38
National Day, 18

national identity, 5, 13, 22, 23, 43
National Stadium, **18**, 19, 41
New Parliament House, 37, **37**
new towns, 24
Ngee Ann City, 26

Old Parliament House, 5
Ong Teng Cheong, 36
orang laut, 9
Orchard Road, 5, 26, **26**

Padang, the, 41
Penang, 9, 10, 27
Peranakan population, 15, 20, 25
petroleum, 33
pirates, 9, 10
political parties, 13, 36
polo, 41
Polo, Marco, 8
polytechnic colleges, 29
pop music, 39
population,10
Portuguese, 9
Pulau Subar Darat, 6
Pulau Subar Laut, 6
Pulau Tekong, 6
Pulau Ubin, 6
Punggol 25

Raffles Cup, 41
Raffles Hotel, 5
Raffles Place, 5, **10**, 34
Raffles, Thomas Stamford, 9, 10,
    10, 16, 27, 37
Ramadan 17, 19
religion, 16–18, 20
restaurants, 20, 21
Ridley, H.N., 11
river people, 9
road travel, 30–31
Robinson Road, 34

Saint Andrew's Cathedral, 17
Sang Nila Utama, 9
schools, 28–29, **29**
Science Hub, 43
Sea nomads, 9
Sentosa Island, 6, 30, 39, 40, **41**
Sepoys, 16
Serangoon Road, 21, 26, 27, 28

Shenton Way, 34
shophouses, 25, 27, **27**
shopping, 5, 26–27
Sikhs, 35
Sindhis, 35
Singapore Art Museum, 39
Singapore Chinese Orchestra, 38
Singapore Conference Hall, 39
Singapore Cup, 41
Singapore Economic Development
    Board (EDB), 35
Singapore History Museum, 39
Singapore Indoor Stadium, 59
Singapore Philatelic Museum, 39
Singapore Polo Club, 41
Singapore Repertory Theatre, 39
Singapore River, 5
Singapore Symphony
    Orchestra, 38
Singapore Turf Club, 41
Singapura, 9
Sisters' Islands, 6
soccer, 41
sports, 40–41
    participation sports, 40–41
    spectator sports, 41
Sri Mariamman Temple, **17**, 18, 20
Strait of Johor, 5
Strait of Malacca, 8, 9
Straits Chinese *see Peranakan*
Suez Canal, 10
Sultan Mosque, 17
Sumatra, 9
Sungei Buloh Nature Park, 6
Supermarkets, 26

Tamils, 8, 16, 20,
Taoism, 16, 17, 20
Teater Kami, 39
Technopreneurship Singapore, 43
Temasek, 8, 9
tennis, 40
Teochews, 14, 35
theaters, 38, 39
Thian Hock Keng Temple, **16**, 17
Thimithi, 20
traffic, 30
trains, 30, **31**
transportation, 25, 30–31, 32, 33
Tua Pek Kong Temple, 20
Tuas, 5, 30

United States, 24, 32
universities, 28, 29–30
Urban Redevelopment Authority
    (URA), 25

Victoria Theatre and Concert
    Hall, 38
volleyball, **41**

water sports, 40–41
water supply, 42–43
Woodlands Causeway, 5, 30
workforce, 35
World of Music, Art and Dance
    (WOMAD) Festival, 39
World War II, 12, 24

Zoroastrianism, 17